Rourke Educational Media
Carson-Dellosa Publishing LLC
PO Box 35665
Greensboro, NC 27425 USA

Printed in China • All rights reserved.
01-271188313

ISBN 978-1-4838-5255-3

TABLE OF CONTENTS

PARENT LETTER

Dear Parents and Caregivers,

You Have a Pet What?! introduces your child to 6 unique and interesting pets. Each section focuses on a different pet and includes:
- an introduction to the pet
- a brief history of the animal
- how to take care of the pet
- behavior and disposition of the animal
- a checklist to determine ability to care for the pet

These pages not only offer all of the fun that comes with having each pet, but also present the responsibilities and challenges associated with each animal.

Each section opens with "Before Reading" questions, giving you the opportunity to prepare your child for the reading. These are questions designed to build and strengthen the following skills:
- reading comprehension
- critical thinking
- vocabulary development
- making connections across the curriculum

The "After Reading" questions from the same page should be asked after each section is complete. These questions are a great tool to help your child build the following skills:
- summarizing
- making inferences
- decision making

Having these tools at hand allows you to insure your child will finish *You Have a Pet What?!* as an avid and curious reader!

YOU HAVE A PET WHAT?!

SKUNK

AUTHOR: ANN MATZKE

LITTLE STINKERS

When you think of skunks do you think, Pee-yew!? A skunk's reputation as a natural stinker **warns** us to stay away. But remove their bad smell, and this boldly striped animal is curious, quick to learn, and tenderhearted.

For some people, skunks make great pets. They can live indoors with humans just like cats and dogs.

▶▶ Close in size to a cat or small dog, skunks weigh about 11 pounds (5 kilograms).

Wild skunks live in North America from Mexico to Canada. There are different types and colors of skunks.

Canada

United States

Mexico

▶▶ The black-and-white striped skunk found in parts of North America is a member of the mephitis mephitis animal family.

Domesticated black and white striped skunks are now bred as pets.

SKUNKS: HEAD TO TOE

eyes ▶

fur ▼

claws ▶

legs ▶

Eyes

The skunk doesn't have great eyesight. It can't see objects more than about 10 feet (3 meters) away.

Fur

A skunk's fur has two layers. The short, curly fur next to their skin keeps them warm. The longer, shiny fur keeps them dry.

Legs

Skunks have stubby legs. They waddle when they walk, but if frightened they can run short distances.

Musk Glands

Under a skunk's tail are two small glands that store the strong-smelling oil. The ends of the glands are like hoses. The skunk will spray the stinky oil when it senses danger.

Paws

A skunk has long, curved claws in front. These claws are important for handling food and digging. The back claws are shorter.

Tail

The skunk's tail is long and bushy. It will raise its tail as a warning.

◄ musk glands

tail

13

BABY SKUNKS

A group of skunks is called a surfeit. Babies
are called kits. A mother skunk gives birth
to a **litter** of five or seven kits
at a time.

At birth, a skunk's eyes are closed. They
have almost no fur, but a black and white
pattern can be seen on their pink skin.

WANT TO OWN A PET SKUNK?

Pet skunks are legal in 17 states. Each state may have different rules, though. Check with your state's authorities before you buy.

Ask your breeder for a health certificate. Save your receipt of payment to prove your skunk was purchased and not from the wild.

Check this map to see if owning a skunk is legal in your state:

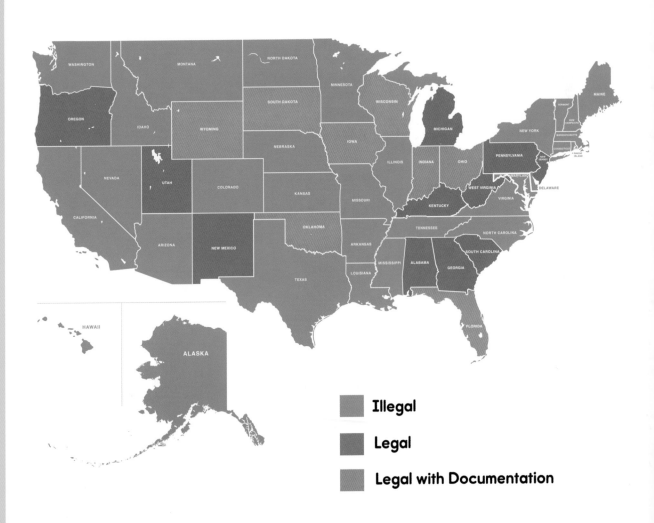

Illegal

Legal

Legal with Documentation

Skunks like to **burrow** and will set up their **den** in a quiet, dark place like a cabinet or a large box. They will build a nest from old towels, blankets or clothing. If you leave things lying around, they might take it for their den!

FUN FACTS

Skunks are nocturnal in the wild but a pet skunk will adapt to your awake and sleep schedule.

Handle your skunk right away. Use your hands for holding and cuddling. Play gently.

PET POINTERS

To avoid a skunk's sharp teeth, use a stuffed animal or a puppet at playtime.

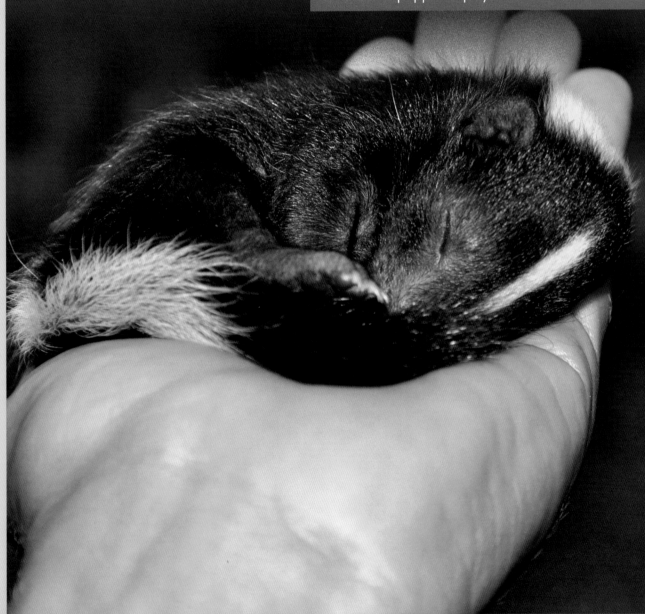

The more you hold, cuddle, and talk to your new skunk the more you are encouraging them to be calm and lovable. Touching their feet, paws, and mouth will help with feeding and trimming claws as they grow older.

Skunks, like any pet, need discipline. It is difficult for skunks to know when they are playing or biting too hard. Never hit or spank. Use the tone and volume of your voice to correct a wrong behavior. Help them understand by using a time-out system to remove them from the situation.

PET POINTERS

Skunks have excellent memories. They never forget being mistreated, and rarely forgive.

▶▶ **Place your pet skunk in a time-out container they can't crawl out of for a few minutes. Stay nearby.**

Skunks are **omnivores**. They eat plants and meat. A skunk's daily diet should be made up of about 40 percent fruits and vegetables, and 60 percent meat and dairy. Skunks have big appetites and may overeat. Discuss a balanced diet and feeding schedule with a veterinarian to prevent obesity.

LITTER TRAINING

Skunks are quite clean and will choose a corner to use as a bathroom. Accept their choice and place several layers of newspaper or an open litter pan with cat litter, wood pellets, or recycled paper. Keep the corner clean or they'll choose a different corner.

KEEPING YOUR SKUNK HEALTHY AND SAFE

Be choosy about a veterinarian. Find one that cares for skunks. Be informed about your skunk's health. Vaccinations are required. All skunks have roundworms and must be treated.

Talk to your veterinarian about removing musk glands and being spayed or neutered. This will help prevent behavior problems later.

PET POINTERS

Skunks will dig where they smell something to eat. They can be destructive, pulling up carpet, digging into wallboard, and scratching at closed doors.

25

A pet skunk is like having a younger brother or sister. Their natural curiosity can lead to danger. Once they know how to do something, they will do it again and again.

Skunk-proof your house: Add safety latches on cabinets. Block the space behind washers and dryers, and refrigerators. Secure vents and windows. Place wastebaskets in secure areas. Remove poisonous products. Be watchful of electric cords and outlets. Never leave windows open.

Skunks don't like water, but can swim if necessary. They do not need a regular bath, but can smell musky at times.

PET POINTERS

Cornmeal can be used like a dry shampoo. Work it into their fur from the tail to the head.

Domesticated pet skunks do not carry the rabies virus. A skunk must be bitten by another animal sick with the rabies virus to become infected. If you have questions, talk to your veterinarian. Consider vaccinating against rabies and know the laws about reporting skunk bites.

SKUNK TALK

Skunks are sensitive animals, full of emotion. They like to communicate their feelings.

Here are some ways skunks communicate:

Happy: **smack their lips**

Wanting attention: **chirp like a bird**

Mad: **squeal or whine**

Sad or frightened: **whimper like a dog**

Upset: **grumble, grunt, or stomp their feet**

When skunks are playing it might look like they are dancing. They'll run forward, stop, stomp their paws, back up, swoosh their tails, and spin around.

Playing is just the beginning of the fun you can have with a pet skunk. Spend time loving and caring for these unique animals and they will love you back.

THINGS TO THINK ABOUT IF YOU WANT A PET SKUNK

- Is it legal to keep a skunk where you live?
- A skunk can live up to ten years. Will you be able to care for it its whole life?
- Do you have a local experienced veterinarian who treats skunks?
- If you have other pets, how will they interact with a skunk?
- Is your home secure enough that your pet won't escape? A skunk can travel several miles a day if it gets loose.
- Pet skunks require a lot of specialized care. Is your family ready to make the commitment?

GLOSSARY

burrow (BUR-oh): a tunnel or hole in the ground made or used by a rabbit, or other animal, such as a skunk

den (den): the home of a wild animal, such as a lion

domesticated (duh-MESS-tuh-kate-ud): something tamed so it can live with or be used by human beings

glands (glands): organs in the body that either produces natural chemicals or allows substances to leave the body, as in sweat glands

legal (LEE-guhl): lawful, or allowed by law

litter (LIT-ur): a group of animals born at the same time to one mother

omnivores (OM-nuh-vorz): animals that eat both plants and meat

rabies (RAY-beez): an often fatal disease that can affect humans, dogs, bats and other warm-blooded animals. Rabies is caused by a virus that attacks the brain and spinal cord and is spread by the bite of an infected animal

warns (worns): tells someone about a danger or a bad thing that might happen

YOU HAVE A PET WHAT?!

BEARDED DRAGON

AUTHOR: CRISTIE REED

DRAGONS: NOT JUST FOR FAIRY TALES

Imagine having a dragon as a best friend. This dragon can crawl up your arm and perch on your shoulder. No worries about breathing fire. This dragon is tame, curious, and funny.

FUN FACTS
Bearded dragons are commonly called beardies.

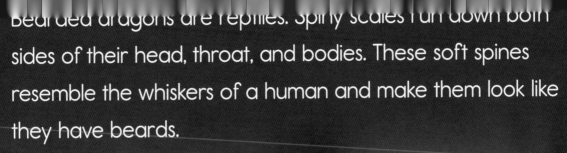

Bearded dragons are reptiles. Spiny scales run down both sides of their head, throat, and bodies. These soft spines resemble the whiskers of a human and make them look like they have beards.

Their size, playful personality, and good temperament make bearded dragons one of the most popular reptiles to keep as pets.

39

BEARDED DRAGONS: HEAD TO TOE

Bearded dragons have a flattened body and triangular-shaped head with ear holes on each side. Rows of teeth run along the top and bottom of their wide mouth. Their long tail equals their body length. Strong legs make them nimble climbers.

FUN FACTS

In the wild, bearded dragons often run on two legs instead of four when they're trying to escape a predator.

ear holes

beard ▶

◀ sharp claws

The bearded dragon puffs out its throat when it feels threatened.

Tail
The tail is about half the length of its body. Unlike other lizards, it will not fall off and grow back.

Ear holes
Beardies do not have external ear structures, just holes. They have excellent hearing. They can press their ears against the ground and hear vibrations.

Claws
Long fingers with claws help beardies climb trees and other structures.

long tail ▶

▶▶ Bearded dragons have feet shaped like human hands. Each toe has a strong claw.

Baby dragons hatch from eggs. The mother digs a hole in sand and lays 11 to 30 oval-shaped eggs. She covers her eggs and leaves them alone to hatch in the warm sand. About two months later, they emerge.

Hatchlings start out two to four inches (5.08 to 10.16 centimeters) long. They reach full size in 12 months. Adults range in size from 12 to 24 inches (30.5 to 60.96 centimeters) and weigh between 12 and 20 ounces (340 to 567 grams). Bearded dragons live up to eight years in the wild. In captivity, they live between 12 and 14 years.

Bearded dragons are typically brown or gray. But many color variations called morphs have been created by breeders. Morphs range in color from red to yellow.

Their skin can be silky smooth or bumpy. While growing, beardies shed their skin every three to four weeks. When full grown, they shed twice per year.

▶▶ **Shedding occurs in patches. Beardies eat less and are less active when shedding.**

LAND OF THE BEARDED DRAGONS

Bearded dragons exist naturally only in the desert regions of Australia. They live throughout the continent, but specific types of dragons vary from place to place. Woodlands, savannahs, and deserts are their natural habitats. They are commonly seen basking on rocks or climbing through trees and bushes.

Bearded dragons were first introduced in the United States in the early 1990s. Some experts speculate that a group of Australian bearded dragons were smuggled into the United States illegally.

Today, any bearded dragon in the U.S. was bred and raised in captivity. Reptile owners consider them to be one of the best lizard pets.

TAKE
ME
HOME!

This reptile enjoys being with humans. Very rarely do they show any aggression. They will sit and relax on a person's body. They enjoy being handled and stroked. They are fairly easy to maintain and don't require walks!

Sit back and watch beardies be themselves. Observe their unique ways of communicating. They make no sound except for some hissing when frightened.

▶▶ Bearded dragons are typically social. Lizards of similar sizes can live together.

Body movements and color changes indicate their moods. Beardies commonly use head-bobbing to show **dominance**. Arm waving shows **submission**. Their beards flare out and darken when they feel threatened or when **mating**. Color changes occur during **rivalry** and temperature changes.

Behavior	What the Bearded Dragon is Saying
Head-bobbing	"I'm the boss." Or "I want to flirt."
Waving	"I'm friendly."
Color Change	"I'm relaxed." Or "I'm feeling stressed."
Gaping Mouth	"Feed me. I'm hungry!"
Beard Puffing	"Watch out! I'm the boss." Or "I want to flirt."
Beard Puffing, Darkening, and Gaping Mouth	"Watch out! I'm getting angry!"
Body Tilting	"See how big I am?"
Biting	"Don't hurt me!" or "I want to flirt."

Baby dragons should be at least six weeks old before they come home with you. Whether you choose a baby or an adult, look for a pet that is plump, alert, and healthy. They should have clean skin and clear eyes.

Beardies can be nervous at first, but they quickly warm up to their humans. When a beardie first comes home, it needs time alone in its new enclosure. Talk to it. Watch to see what it wants to do. Your pet needs to know you are not a threat.

Let your pet get to know you. Gently stroke the beardie along its head and back. You want your bearded dragon to get used to you holding and petting it, but start slowly. Offer it food treats as rewards.

HAPPY, HEALTHY BEARDIES

A healthy dragon is a happy dragon. These **omnivores** have hearty appetites and special **nutritional** requirements. They require a balance of live insects and leafy, green vegetables.

Insects must be raised especially for pet consumption. Offer only clean, fresh vegetables. Feed fresh fruits as a snack. In captivity, their diet needs to be supplemented with vitamins and calcium D3.

PET POINTERS

Dust insects with calcium before feeding them to your beardie.

▶▶ **Bearded dragons can eat some flowers and flower petals.**

Adult dragons need 80 percent leafy greens and 20 percent insects. Feed adults once or twice daily. Baby dragons need 80 percent insects and 20 percent greens. Feed babies several times a day.

▶▶ Insects and vegetables should be small enough to fit between the lizard's eyes. Food that is too large could cause choking.

FOODS TO KEEP YOUR BEARDED DRAGON HEALTHY

Recommended Insects

black soldier fly larvae
butterworms
crickets
Dubia roaches
earthworms
locusts
redworms
superworms

Recommended Vegetables

artichoke hearts
bell peppers
bok choy
butternut squash
cabbage
celery
collard greens
dandelion greens
endive
kale
mustard greens
peeled cucumber
yellow squash

Fruit for Occasional Snacks

apples
apricots
bananas
grapes
kiwi
mangos
melon
peaches
pears
plums
strawberries

PET POINTERS

Foods to Avoid: Beardies should not eat lettuce, spinach, avocadoes, insects from the wild, or fireflies. Bearded dragons, especially babies, should not consume mealworms.

Dangerous for Dragons: There are many plants and flowers that can be harmful or poisonous for bearded dragons. Check with a reptile specialist to learn more about unsafe foods.

Dragons have special requirements for **hydration**. They take in water through their skin, so they need soaking or misting often. They need a constant supply of fresh water for drinking. Regular baths allow them to soak and drink at the same time.

▶▶ Use a soft toothbrush to gently scrub the dragon during bathtime.

A proper indoor **environment** should mimic their natural habitat. Special reptile cages ensure proper safety, temperature, and lighting.

Beardies need 12 to 14 hours of light during the day and no light at night. Reptiles need both UVA and UVB light rays. Proper lighting promotes digestion and warmth for basking. Temperatures should be 80 to 85 degrees Fahrenheit (26.7 to 29.4 degrees Celsius) during the day and 70 to 74 degrees Fahrenheit (21.1 to 23.3 degrees Celsius) at night.

Like all pets, bearded dragons need regular check-ups from a veterinarian. Expect the vet to examine their eyes, mouth, and skin to see if anything looks wrong. Beardies need yearly checks for signs of internal parasites.

PET POINTERS

Bearded dragons have a cloaca, or vent, for releasing urine and feces. A vet will check this vent to be sure it is not clogged.

PROTECTION FOR BEARDED DRAGONS

Australia has strict laws to protect bearded dragons. In the 1960s, they banned the sale of wild bearded dragons to the pet industry. Beardies cannot be taken from the wild. In Australia, pet owners need a license to keep a bearded dragon as a pet.

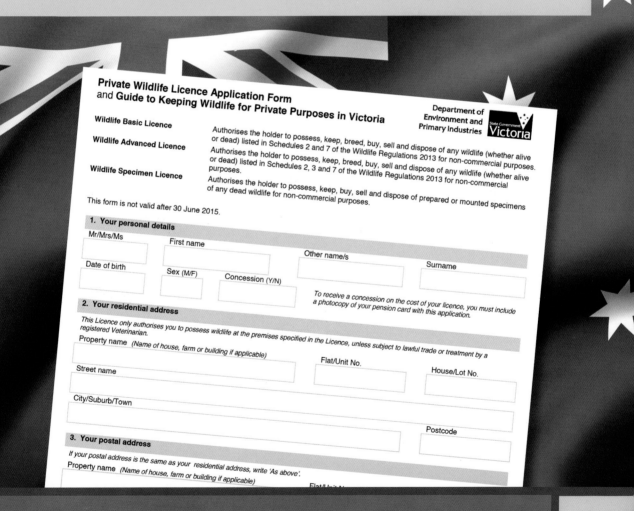

In the United States, bearded dragons must be **captive** bred only. People who breed or sell these animals must have a permit. Bearded dragons should never be released into the wild. This would be cruel to the animal and a threat to the environment.

THINGS TO THINK ABOUT IF YOU WANT A BEARDED DRAGON

- Male bearded dragons should be housed alone to prevent fighting with other males and breeding with females.
- Bearded dragons live up to 14 years in captivity.
- Pet owners need a fairly large indoor area for the bearded dragon's enclosure.
- Dragons need UVA and UVB light. Their habitat needs to be kept at proper temperatures.
- Equipment and supplies for their indoor habitat can be costly.
- Bearded dragons thrive on a daily routine for feeding, light, hydration, and attention.
- Environmental needs make traveling difficult.
- Bearded dragons can carry a disease called salmonella. Always wash hands before and after handling.

GLOSSARY

basking (BASK-ing): to lie or sit in the sunshine and enjoy it

captive (KAP-tiv): captured and held in a cage

dominance (DOM-uh-nuhns): to show power or control

environment (en-VYE-ruhn-muhnt): your surroundings; all things that influence your life

hatchlings (HACH-lings): recently hatched animals

hydration (hye-DRAY-shun): to supply enough moisture or water

mating (MAT-ing): to join together for breeding

nutritional (noo-TRISH-uh-nuhl): provides substances that the body can use to stay strong and healthy

omnivores (OM-ni-vorz): animals that live on a diet of both plants and animals

rivalry (RYE-vuhl-ree): a competition between two creatures

submission (sub-MISH-uhn): to obey someone or something

temperament (TEM-pur-uh-muhnt): your nature or personality; the way you usually think, act or respond

YOU HAVE A PET WHAT?!

HEDGEHOG
AUTHOR: ANN MATZKE

WHAT KIND OF ANIMAL?

What animal gets its name from the shrubbery it searches for food and the pig-like grunting sound it makes?
A hedgehog.

Hedgehogs are not your typical pet. These interesting and unusual **nocturnal** animals with bright eyes, sweet faces, and prickly backs require special care and handling. Knowing more about hedgehogs will help you decide if it is the right pet for you.

DAYS OF THE DINOSAURS

Hedgehogs are one of the oldest, most **primitive** animals to roam the Earth since the time of dinosaurs.

Imagine these little animals sniffing and snuffling as they **waddle** along behind woolly mammoths or saber-toothed tigers. Not much has changed for the hedgehog since the days of its prehistoric relatives.

Hedgehogs are native to Europe, Asia, and Africa. The African Pygmy is the most common species kept as pets.

FUN FACTS

There are 17 species of hedgehogs in the world. The most common pet species is the African Pygmy hedgehog. Other types kept as pets include the long-eared hedgehog and the Indian long-eared hedgehog.

Originally from Northern and Central Africa, they are at home in grasslands, savannahs, and scrub areas.

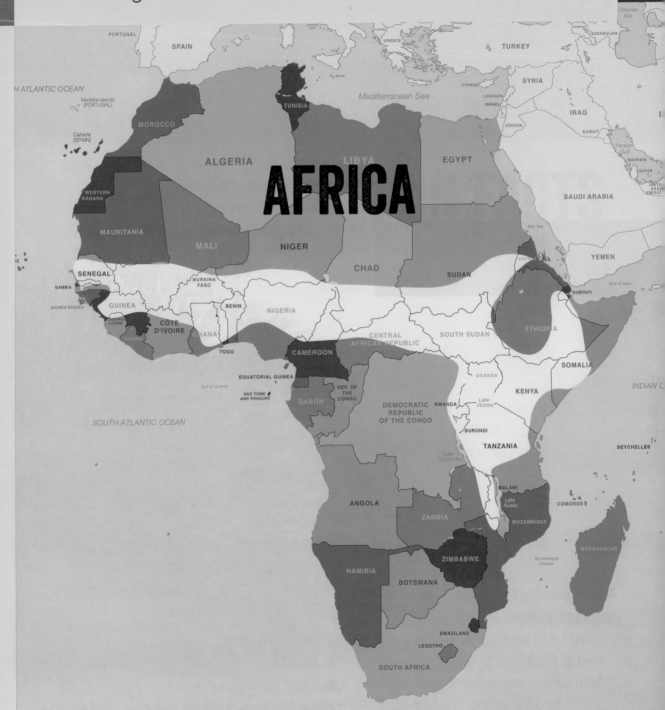

CURLING INTO A BALL

Muscles under the edge of a hedgehog's spiny coat control the position of the quills. A frightened hedgehog can roll into a ball, drawing the edges of its spiny coat together like a drawstring, with its head, belly, and feet tucked inside. The quills are not barbed or poisonous. They crisscross and offer protection from predators and falls. The quills also help it blend into its environment.

▶▶ **Hedgehogs have an average of 5,000 to 7,000 quills.**

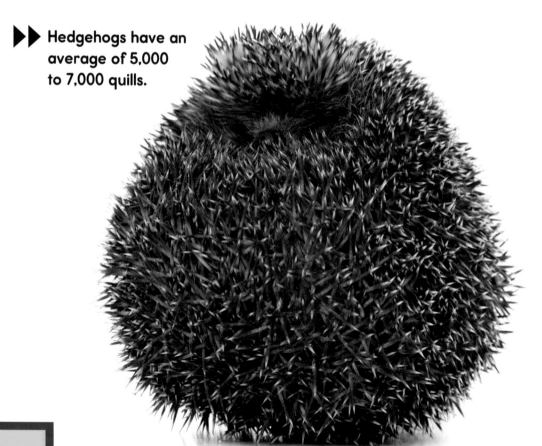

QUILLS

Quills are stiff hairs. They are thick, hollow on the inside, and lightweight. They are short, measuring from a quarter inch to one inch long (0.5 to 2.5 centimeters). Quills are smooth to touch but can be sharp on the ends. Quills grow out of the skin and don't come loose. Adult hedgehog quills are permanent. Removal may injure the animal.

FUN FACTS

Young hedgehogs lose the quills they are born with, replacing them with adult spines. This process is called quilling.

IS A HEDGEHOG THE RIGHT PET?

Some states, counties, and districts do not allow hedgehogs as pets. Before buying one, check with local authorities. Even if it's legal to own a hedgehog you might need to buy a permit.

Local animal control agencies or your state's fish and wildlife department can help with permits.

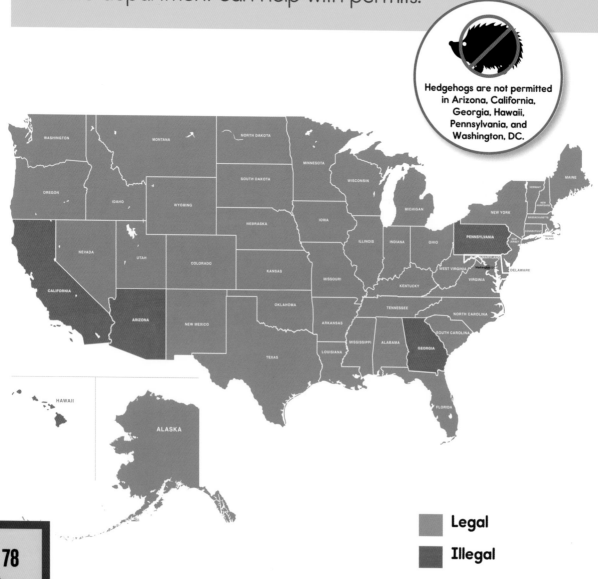

Hedgehogs are not permitted in Arizona, California, Georgia, Hawaii, Pennsylvania, and Washington, DC.

Legal

Illegal

WHAT TO LOOK FOR WHEN SELECTING A HEDGEHOG

Hedgehogs are not your typical pet. These interesting and unusual **nocturnal** animals with bright eyes, sweet faces, and prickly backs require special care and handling. Knowing more about hedgehogs will help you decide if it is the right pet for you.

FUN FACTS

Hedgehogs can be litter trained like cats.

HOME SWEET HOME

Hedgehogs are solitary animals, which means they like to live alone. The scent of a dog or cat nearby can stress them out.

PET POINTERS

A pet hedgehog needs:
- an indoor rabbit cage or hutch without wire bottom
- a dark place to sleep and burrow, or a sleeping hut
- safe, easy to clean cage liner made from washable cloth or paper pellets
- heavy crock or bottle for water
- large exercise wheel
- heavy food bowl to prevent tipping
- plenty of places to hide
- a shallow litter box, open on one end and filled with pellet paper litter

African Pygmy hedgehogs come from a warm climate. They need the room temperature to be consistently between 75 and 80 degrees Fahrenheit (24 to 27 degrees Celsius).

A hedgehog's cage should be placed somewhere to receive 12 hours of daylight and 12 hours of darkness. They have sensitive ears so find a quiet, out of the way spot for the cage.

At night, when hedgehogs are awake, they are on the move. Don't let them get bored. A pet hedgehog needs plenty of toys, tubes, and hideaways to explore.

WELCOME TO THE FAMILY

Moving-in day can be stressful for hedgehogs. Keep noises down and speak softly. Introduce new things slowly.

Spend time getting to know one another. Friendly hedgehogs are handled often. Your hedgehog will soon recognize you by your scent.

PET POINTERS

You can help your hedgehog get to know your scent by wearing a T-shirt all day then draping it over your pet's cage.

▶▶ New lotions and perfumes can confuse your hedgehog because they cover up your original scent.

HANDLING A HEDGEHOG

Handle your hedgehog when it is awake. Be quiet and slow. Pick it up with your hands, not gloves. Put a hand on each side of your pet and slowly bring them together.

Set your new pet in your lap or another safe place in case it wiggles free. It may be shy at first. Be patient and gentle. Talk in a calm, quiet voice. Gently stroking it will help it relax. Reward your pet with a treat for good behavior.

STAYING FIT AND HEALTHY

Hedgehogs grow to be six to eight inches (15 to 20 centimeters) long and weigh 18 to 25 ounces (.51 to .70 kilograms). They live an average of five to eight years.

Hedgehogs need a balanced diet. Their daily intake should include:

- dry, hard food
- a few live insects as a treat
- a small amount of fresh fruits and vegetables

Consult a veterinarian about the specifics of your pet's diet.

▶▶ **Do not leave food out all day. Feed your hedgehog in the morning and evening when it is awake and most active.**

FINDING A VETERINARIAN

It is important to find a veterinarian who is knowledgeable and cares for hedgehogs. Ask for recommendations when purchasing your hedgehog.

Keep the phone number handy for a 24-hour veterinary clinic in case of an emergency. If your hedgehog becomes ill or is injured, you want to seek medical help quickly.

89

BEHAVIOR

Hedgehogs are fast runners, good climbers, explorers, and escape artists. Make sure your pet's cage is safe and secure.

▶▶ Hedgehogs like to hide in warm, dark places. To find a hiding hedgehog, get on your hands and knees and explore under and behind appliances and furniture.

- spray bottle
- gentle hypo-allergenic shampoo
- soft toothbrush
- smooth towel

GROOMING

Hedgehogs keep themselves fairly clean but occasionally you might need to give your pet a bath. In a small sink or basin, place your pet in about an inch of warm water. Using a spray bottle, spray warm water on the quills and gently clean the skin and quills with shampoo and a soft toothbrush. Rinse well, being careful to not get water or shampoo in its eyes, ears, nose, or mouth. Wrap your hedgehog in a smooth towel to dry. When the bath is over, reward your pet with a treat.

SELF-ANOINTING

When hedgehogs smell or taste something strange, they can make a frothy saliva in their mouth. They'll spread the saliva across their quills with their long tongues. This is called self-anointing.

Sometimes it will be a couple of licks and other times they may spend several minutes covering their quills.

Hedgehogs do this to smell like the new object. They also may cover themselves this way to cool down or protect themselves from something.

If the hedgehog doesn't clean off the dried saliva, you may need to give it a bath.

FUN FACTS

Self-anointing is when an animal smears secretions or parts of other animals or plants on itself.

THINGS TO THINK ABOUT IF YOU WANT A PET HEDGEHOG

- Can you have a hedgehog where you live?
- Can you provide the equipment needed?
- Do you have time to care for and interact with a hedgehog?
- Can you make the commitment for six to eight years?

They may not be soft and cuddly like kittens or puppies, but hedgehogs are fascinating pets.

GLOSSARY

drawstring (DRAW-string): a string or cord that closes or tightens a bag or piece of clothing when you pull the ends

frothy (frawthee): lots of small bubbles in or on top of a liquid

high frequency (hye FREE-kwuhn-see): higher pitched sounds

nocturnal (nok-TUR-nuhl): to do with the night or happening at night

permit (pur-MIT): to allow something

predators (PRED-uh-turz): animals that hunt other animals for food

primitive (PRIM-uh-tiv): an early stage of development

savannahs (suh-VAN-uhs): flat grassy plains with few trees or no trees in tropical areas

snout (snout): the long, front part of an animal's head

solitary (SOL-uh-ter-ee): prefers to be alone

waddle (WAHD-uhl): to walk awkwardly, taking short steps and swaying from side to side

YOU HAVE A PET WHAT?!

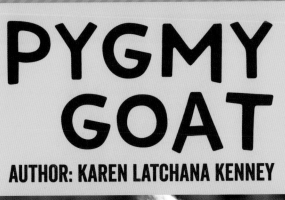

PYGMY GOAT

AUTHOR: KAREN LATCHANA KENNEY

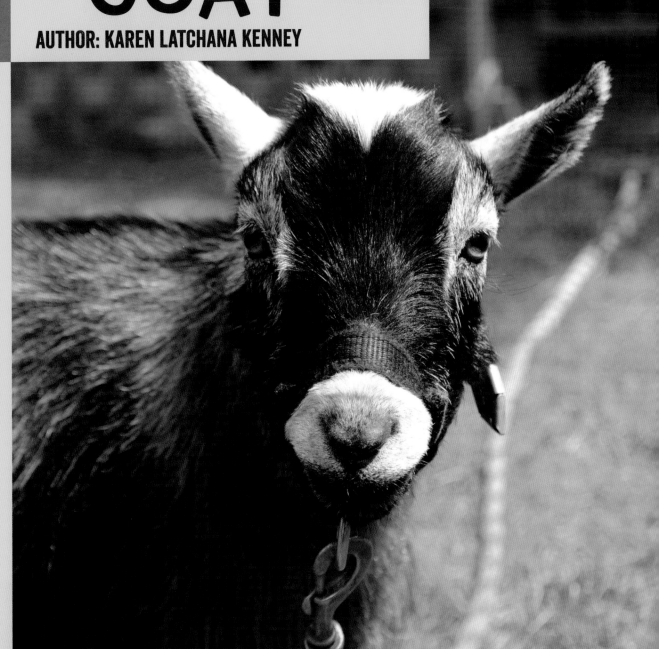

BEFORE & AFTER READING ACTIVITIES

BEFORE READING:

Building Academic Vocabulary and Background Knowledge

Before reading a book, it is important to tap into what your child or students already know about the topic. This will help them develop their vocabulary, increase their reading comprehension, and make connections across the curriculum.

1. Look at the cover of the section. What will this reading be about?
2. What do you already know about the topic?
3. Let's study the Table of Contents. What will you learn about in this section's chapters?
4. What would you like to learn about this topic? Do you think you might learn about it from this book? Why or why not?
5. Use a reading journal to write about your knowledge of this topic. Record what you already know about the topic and what you hope to learn about the topic.
6. Read the section.
7. In your reading journal, record what you learned about the topic and your response to the section.
8. After reading the section complete the activities below.

Content Area Vocabulary
Read the list. What do these words mean?

bond
breeders
disbudding
domesticated
forage
herd
kids
mammal
predators
ruminants
vaccinations
vegetarian
veterinarian

AFTER READING:

Comprehension and Extension Activity

After reading the section, work on the following questions with your child or students in order to check their level of reading comprehension and content mastery.

1. Where should pet pygmy goats live? (Summarize)
2. Why do you think some owners remove their pygmy goat's horns? (Infer)
3. What food do pygmy goats forage for? (Asking questions)
4. Do you think a pygmy goat would be a good pet for your family? Why? (Text to self connection)
5. What might happen if you don't take care of a pygmy goat's hooves? (Asking questions)

Extension Activity
Pygmy goats are domesticated animals. Pick another kind of domesticated animal to research, such as a cow, horse, dog, or cat. What wild animal is its ancestor? When did humans domesticate this animal?

TABLE OF CONTENTS

HAPPY KIDS

It's morning on the farm and two young pygmy goats are ready for some fun! The cute kids jump onto a tree stump, wagging their tails. Then they hop off, kicking their legs high into the air.

FUN FACTS

Kids just practice head butting. But for adults, head butting shows strength and power in a **herd**.

They stand up on their hind legs. They fall forward and butt heads. But the kids aren't hurt. They're just playing. Pygmy goats love to play and explore. Their cute looks, small size, and playful personalities make them popular pets.

Pet pygmy goats come from breeders. But this small animal originally came from West Africa.

A pygmy goat is a domesticated animal. Its distant relative is the wild Bezoar goat. People trained wild goats to be tame over thousands of years. That's how they became farm animals.

Wild Beezer Goat

FUN FACTS

Goats can live 10 to 14 years. The oldest known goat lived more than 22 years!

The pygmy goat is also called the Cameroon Dwarf Goat. It comes from the country of Cameroon. Herds are now in many parts of West Africa. In West Africa, the pygmy goat is raised mostly for its meat, but it also makes milk. The first pygmy goats to leave Africa went to zoos in Sweden and Germany. They first came to the United States in 1959.

▶▶ ■ West Africa

PYGMY GOATS: HEAD TO TOE

What's so cute about pygmy goats? They're not just tiny. They have short legs, a big forehead, and a large, round body. They look like baby goats even as adults. They grow to just 16 to 22 inches (41 to 56 centimeters) tall. That's about the size of a dog. This small mammal also has many other unique features.

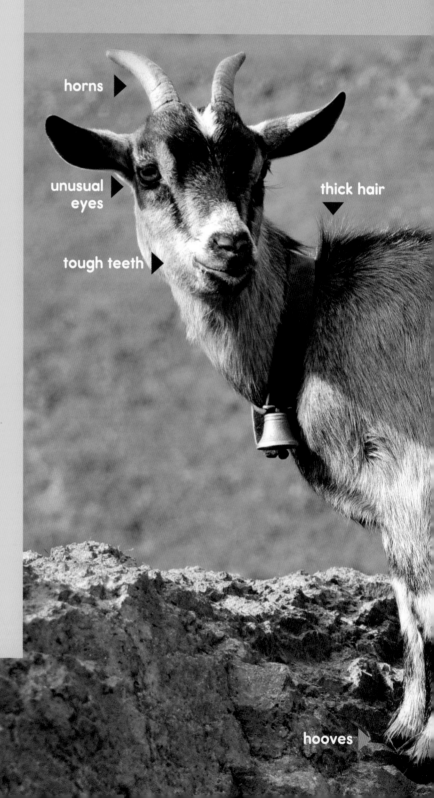

horns ▶

unusual eyes ▶

thick hair ▼

tough teeth ▶

hooves ▶

Two bony horns grow from a pygmy goat's head. Horns help keep goats cool by letting off body heat. Goats also protect themselves from predators with their horns.

Thick Hair

Pygmy goats have medium to long, straight hair. It gets thicker in colder areas or seasons. Males have long, full beards and a mane.

Hooves

Hard hooves have two toes. Hooves make pygmy goats great climbers.

Tail

Its short tail sticks up and wags back and forth.

Tough Teeth

Pygmy goats chew a lot of tough plants. They have grinding teeth in the back of their mouths. At the front, they only have teeth on their lower jaw. The top jaw just has hard gums at the front.

Unusual Eyes

A goat's eye pupils aren't round. They're rectangular! This lets them see far at the sides of their head while eating plants by the ground.

tail

PET PYGMIES

Why would you pick a goat as a pet? Pygmy goats have unique, playful personalities. They're easy to care for, and they get along well with people and other animals. Some owners walk their pet pygmy goats on leashes, just like dogs. These pets bond well with owners. They love to cuddle. Some even sit on their owners' laps.

NIGERIAN DWARF GOATS

You can choose another kind of miniature goat as a pet. A Nigerian Dwarf goat is cute too. It looks like a regular goat, just much smaller. It is a dairy goat. That means it needs to be milked at least twice a day.

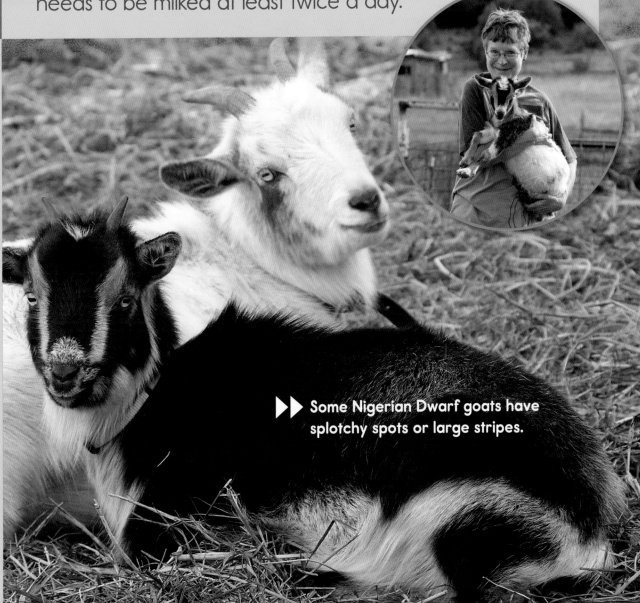

▶▶ Some Nigerian Dwarf goats have splotchy spots or large stripes.

You may want to pick female pygmies. Males can be harder to care for. They pee on their legs and beards. They try to attract females. They can be a little smelly. But a neutered male mixes well with female goats. It doesn't try to attract them.

Horns can be a problem too. Pygmy goats may get excited and accidently poke you, causing a serious injury. Goats can also destroy fences. Some owners choose to remove their pet's horns. This is called disbudding, which must be done when pygmy goats are only two weeks old.

You can buy a pygmy goat from a breeder. Ask the breeder about the goat's health and find out what vaccinations it has had. A goat rescue farm is another great option. These goats may have been neglected or abused. Or their owners couldn't afford to keep them. Adopt a pygmy goat to give it a new chance at having a happy home.

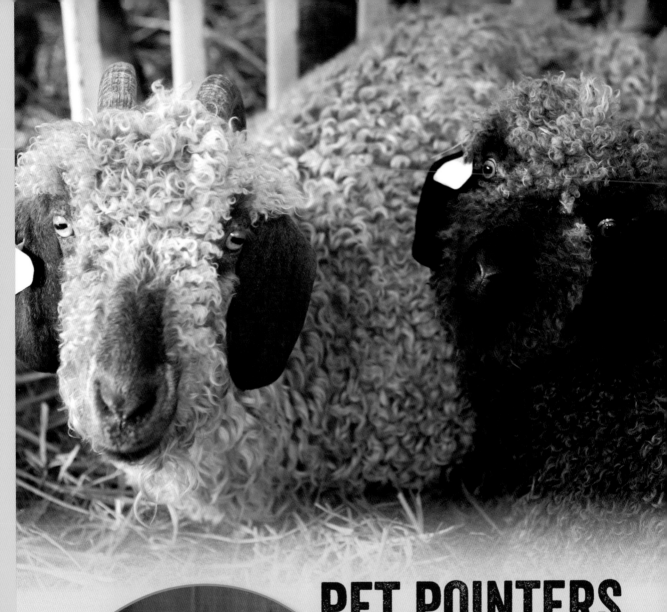

PET POINTERS

You can take your pygmy goat home when it is 12 to 14 weeks old. Make sure it looks healthy. It should have bright eyes, be alert, and its tail should be sticking up.

▶▶ A pygora is a mix of a pygmy goat and an Angora goat. It was bred for its coat, which is full and curly.

111

CARING FOR YOUR PET PYGMY

Pygmy goats need a big area enclosed by a good fence. Goats are great at escaping. Build a fence at least 4 feet (1.2 meters) tall. Use wooden posts and wire mesh.

Your pet pygmy needs a dry, draft-free outdoor shelter that lets in fresh air. Solid wood is best. Goats like to chew on things and chemicals might be in other materials.

A 6-by-8-foot (1.8-by-2.4-meter) shed fits two pygmy goats. Line the floor with straw or wood shavings. A bench makes a nice bed for a pygmy goat. Put a concrete or paved area by the shed. Pygmy goats don't like to get muddy. They can stand on the hard area to stay dry and clean.

A pygmy goat's hooves grow like fingernails. They need to be trimmed every four to six weeks. If they get too long, your goat will limp. Its feet will hurt. It might get hoof rot, an infection of the hooves. Use hoof trimmers to make hooves flat.

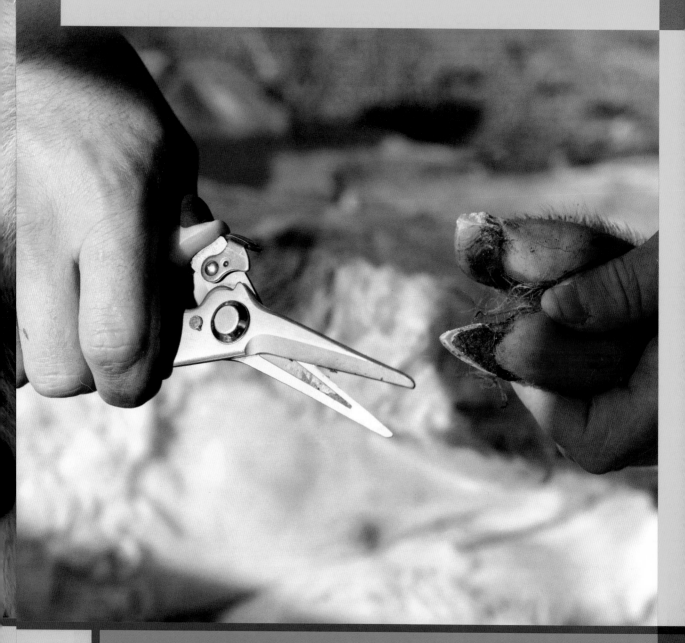

Does your goat look sick? Is it thin? Is it coughing? It might have worms in its intestines. That's common in goats. You need a good veterinarian for your pet. Make sure your pet gets the vaccinations and care it needs to stay healthy.

PET POINTERS

Sometimes goats eat too much grain or spring grass, which can lead to bloat. This is a buildup of gases in its stomachs. Your goat's left side will bulge. It's very serious. Without treatment, bloat could kill your pet.

If it's not used to people, a pygmy goat can be a nervous pet. Spend as much time as you can with your goats. This is especially important when you first bring them home.

Try quietly reading a book to your goats. Take them into their shed at night and put them to bed. Bring them some hay to eat. Pet your new friends. They will start to know you. They will be comfortable around other people, too.

One of the best parts about being a pygmy goat owner is watching your pets play! Make them a playground. Give your goats lots of things to climb up, jump off, and run around. Old tractor tires and logs are great. Make a teeter totter with a board and a log. A trampoline is fun too. Just make sure the springs are covered so your goats won't hurt their legs.

Teach your pets some simple tricks. Train them to shake hands, spin in a circle, or weave between your legs. Give your goats healthy treats as rewards.

PET POINTERS

Healthy goat treats include:
- raisins
- popped popcorn
- sunflower seeds
- chopped apples and pears

Pygmy goats make wonderful pets. They're always curious and playful. They are loving friends to other animals and people. And they're fun to watch! Give your pygmy goats enough space to roam. Build them a nice home. They will become your new best friends!

THINGS TO THINK ABOUT IF YOU WANT A PYGMY GOAT

- Pygmy goats can be noisy and smelly. Your neighbors might not like them living next door.
- Different cities and states have laws about keeping pygmy goats. Make sure it is okay where you live.
- You need to own at least two pygmy goats. They do not do well as single pets.
- It is important to have space outside for your pets. Pygmy goats need a dry shelter and fenced area to roam.
- Owners should trim their goats' hooves every four to six weeks.

MEET THE MINI

When you come home to a dog or cat you are greeted by barks, meows, and wagging tails. Keep the wagging tails and substitute snorts, grunts, or squeals – that is the happy greeting you receive when you come home to a mini pig. Miniature, potbellied, micro, pocket, and teacup are names for a type of dwarf swine bred to be smaller than a domestic farm pig. Their good temperament and small size have made them popular pets in North America and Europe.

▶▶ Pigs are fast learners. A scientist once taught pigs to play video games!

Mini piglets come into the world no bigger than a kitten. They grow quickly. An adult may weigh about 100 pounds (45 kilograms). They stand about 18 inches (45 centimeters) high at the shoulder. Depending on the breed and the size of their parents, they may grow larger or smaller. Their typical lifespan is 10 to 15 years. Some mini pig breeds can live longer.

FUN FACTS

A full-grown mini pig's weight is compact. A 100 pound (45 kilogram) pig may be the same size as a 50 pound (23 kilogram) dog.

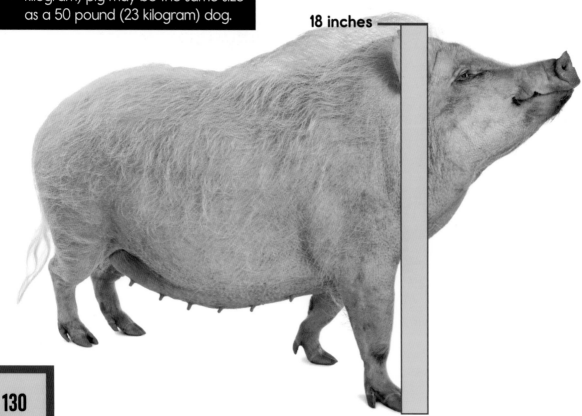

18 inches

Just like farm pigs, mini pigs are known for their chubby round bodies, flat noses, and curly tails. Their large ears stand up straight and their small, dark eyes are protected by long lashes. They have thick, strong snouts for rooting and digging. On each foot they have a hoof. Their tails can be curly, straight, or kinked.

Mini pigs have some distinctive characteristics. They will never grow as large as a typical farm pig. They may have a swayed back and an oversized belly that makes them look like they've eaten too much. Their legs are usually short, which makes their bellies nearly touch the ground.

FUN FACTS

Pigs are cloven-hoofed, which means their hoof is split into two toes. They walk on two front toes and have two back toes called dewclaws.

MANY BREEDS OF MINI PIGS

Mini Pig Breeds	Adult Weight	Color	Unique Characteristics	Photo
Vietnamese potbellied pig or potbellied pig	90-150 pounds (40-68 kilograms)	solid black, white, or a mix of both	swayed back, potbelly, wrinkled skin, short turned up nose, straight tail	
Guinea hog or African pygmy	100-300 pounds (45-135 kilograms)	black	straight back, short legs, short snout, kinky tail, bristly coat	
Ossabaw Island pig or feral pigs	40-90 pounds (18-40 kilograms)	solid gray, blue, or red; spotted black and white, calico	straight back and belly, long snout, medium ears, heavy coat	
Juliana pig or painted miniature	50 pounds (22 kilograms)	solid red, black, silver, white, or a mix of two colors	longer legs, slight potbelly, small ears, straight tail	
Göttigen	50-100 pounds (22-45 kilograms)	pink and black	straight back and belly, sparse hair, short snout, medium ears	
Kunekune	70 pounds (31 kilograms)	solid black, gold, tan, brown, or black and white	straight back, rounded belly, short legs, short upturned nose, curly tail, tassels that hang from lower jaw	

ONCE UPON A TIME

Mini pigs have existed on different continents around the world for hundreds of years. Ancestors of mini pigs were brought to North America by early settlers as a source of food. In Europe, mini pigs were bred for medical research before they became popular as pets.

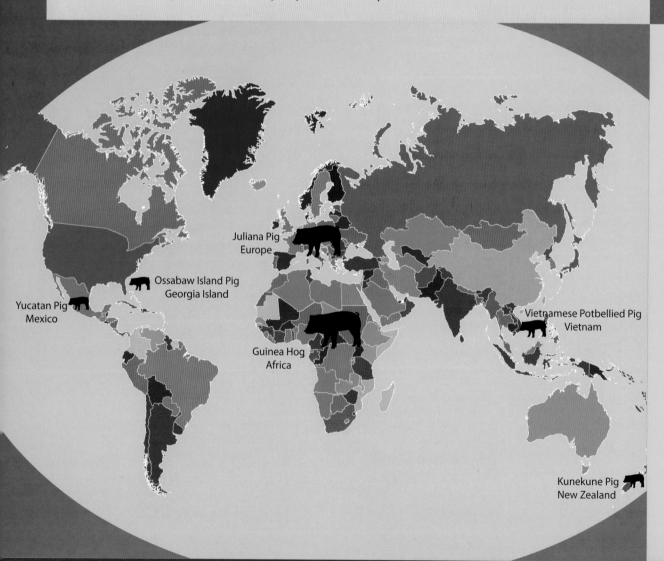

Juliana Pig
Europe

Ossabaw Island Pig
Georgia Island

Yucatan Pig
Mexico

Vietnamese Potbellied Pig
Vietnam

Guinea Hog
Africa

Kunekune Pig
New Zealand

A young woman and her pet pig pose for a photo in the 1920s.

Vietnamese potbellied pigs were imported to North America by a Canadian zookeeper in the 1980s. That specific group of pigs was bred and their offspring were sent to zoos in the United States. When people saw them, they quickly fell in love with the petite pigs. They thought they might make great pets. More attention came to mini pigs when wealthy people and celebrities began purchasing them. The popularity of these exotic pigs spread rapidly in the 1980s.

GOING WHOLE HOG

Mini pigs have unique personalities. They can be quirky and lovable, but sometimes stubborn or pig-headed. They are extremely curious and very intelligent. They use their squeals, snorts, and grunts to show happiness and communicate their needs. When they want something, you will hear about it!

▶▶ **Pigs have excellent memories.**

It is in the pig's nature to use its thick, strong snout to root and dig. Wallowing on their backs and scratching with their hooves is also normal pig behavior. Pigs love to eat. Some clever pigs have learned to open refrigerators and cupboards to get a treat!

▶▶ **You can find tips and tricks for training your mini pig on the Internet.**

Pigs are social animals. Mini pigs like lots of attention and enjoy the companionship of their humans and other pigs. They develop a strong and trusting bond with their owners. They run, jump, and play with children and other pets. They like to give and receive affection. Mini pigs snuggle with their humans on the couch or curl up with them in bed. They are in hog heaven when they get a back rub or a belly scratch. They love a good bath.

A Pig-tionary

boar: a male pig
hog: a larger pig
litter: a group of piglets born to a sow
pettitoes: a tiny pig's feet
pig: common term for a younger animal
piggy: a sow late in her pregnancy
piggery: a place where pigs are kept
piglet: a baby pig from birth to eight weeks of age
runt: the smallest piglet in a litter
sow: a female pig

FUN FACTS

In the animal world, pigs are among the most intelligent creatures. Their intelligence ranks just behind apes, monkeys, whales, and dolphins.

THIS LITTLE PIGGY

Mini piglets need to stay with their mother until they are eight weeks old. When they arrive in the home as pets, they need their own space. They will naturally be frightened and need time to get used to their new environment. Provide an area separate from humans and other pets. The piglet needs to feel safe and secure. This is how it can start to develop trust with its new family members.

▶▶ **A dog or cat bed will also work well for your mini pig.**

To become a good pet, proper socialization is critical. It takes love, patience, and time to get to know your new pet. Gradually introduce yourself and other family members to the young pig. Some piglets are not fond of being picked up or held. They use their high-pitched squeal to let you know when they are afraid.

FUN FACTS

Piglets are among the noisiest of all babies! Their squeals can reach 115 decibels. That's as loud as a rock concert!

EVERYTHING'S PIGGY!

The mini piglet needs a pen with a bed in its new home. A playpen works well. Provide lots of blankets and towels for rooting and burrowing. They enjoy having a few soft toys to push around with their snouts. Mini piglets need special baby food and plenty of water for drinking. Put a litter box in their pen. They can start to use it right away.

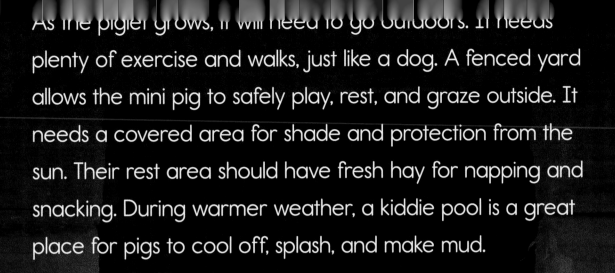

As the piglet grows, it will need to go outdoors. It needs plenty of exercise and walks, just like a dog. A fenced yard allows the mini pig to safely play, rest, and graze outside. It needs a covered area for shade and protection from the sun. Their rest area should have fresh hay for napping and snacking. During warmer weather, a kiddie pool is a great place for pigs to cool off, splash, and make mud.

PET POINTERS

White or light-colored pigs fare better in warm, sunny climates. Dark-colored pigs fare better in cooler, less sunny climates.

Indoor pigs need a safe space that is pig-proof. Set up gates to keep the mini pig contained in its area. Keep dangerous objects such as cords and plastic bags off the floor. Cover slick floors with cloth or rugs.

PET POINTERS

One of the benefits of owning a mini pig is that they don't shed. They have hair, not fur. This makes them good pets for people with pet allergies. Another benefit is that they seldom get fleas.

Mini pigs must be fed a high-quality pig chow to get protein and important nutrients. They need fresh raw vegetables such as potatoes, carrots, and lettuce. Find out how much food is right and set up a feeding schedule. Be careful of overfeeding a mini pig because it could gain too much weight.

▶▶ A dip in mud can lower a pig's temperature by 3.6 degrees Fahrenheit (2 degrees Celsius).

FUN FACTS

As Happy as a Pig in Mud!
Pigs have an undeserved reputation for being filthy animals. But their slovenliness can be attributed to the fact that they have no sweat glands and they are easily sunburned. They roll in mud to cool off and protect themselves from the sun.

WHEN PIGS FLY!

We will never actually see a pig fly, but they can learn to do some amazing feats. Mini pigs are very trainable and have good memories. Mini pigs can learn to ride skateboards, run in races, and jump through hoops. They learn their names very quickly and respond well to commands such as "Come" or "Sit."

▶▶ Mini pig races are popular at many fairs and festivals.

Mini pigs learn best with positive reinforcement. Pigs love to eat, so training treats, such as fruit, make great rewards for correct behavior. They also respond to the tone of your voice and affection. Never use force with a mini pig. Just like dogs and cats, mini pigs can be housebroken or potty trained. They can be taught to walk on a leash and can travel in the car.

▶▶ **After you've bonded with your pet, you can teach it all kinds of tricks.**

RESPONSIBLE MINI PIG OWNERSHIP

When considering mini pig ownership, look for a caring and knowledgeable mini pig breeder. Try to see the mini pig's parents to determine the pig's eventual size and overall well-being.

PET POINTERS

The cost of a mini pig can range from $800 to $1,000 or more.

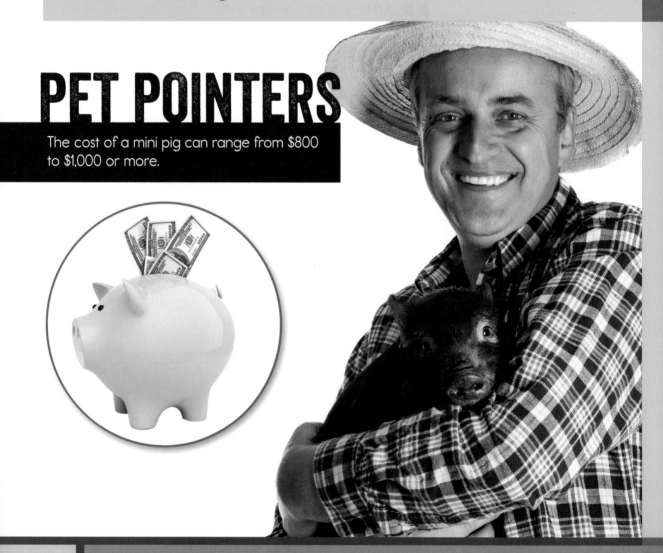

Look for a good temperament. The mini pig should be active and energetic. It should not be too fat. It should have clear eyes and straight, clean teeth. Their hooves should be trimmed and free from damage.

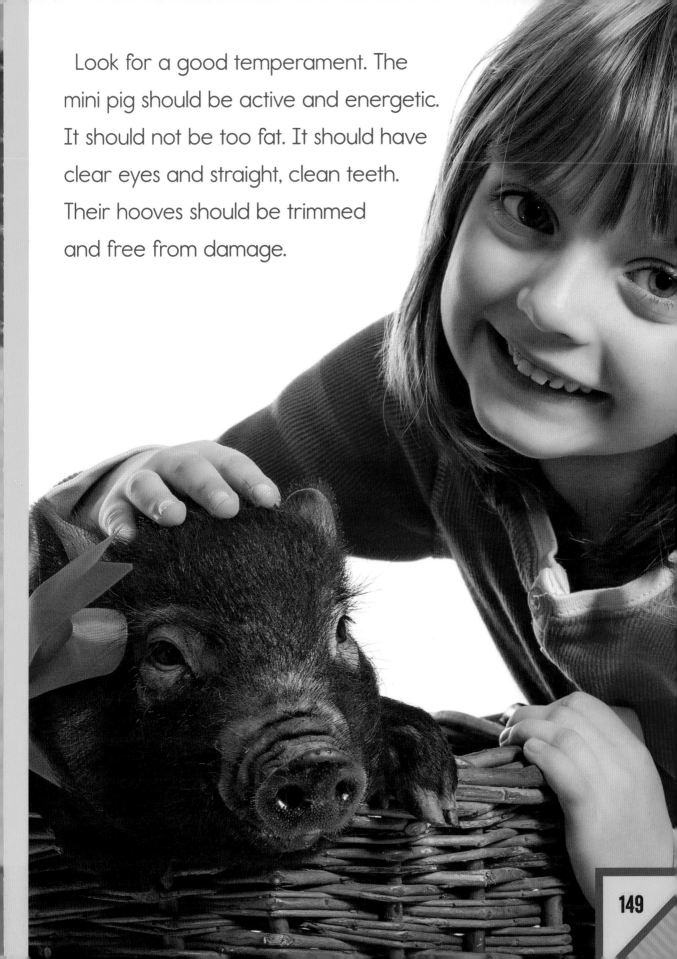

Owning a mini pig is not legal in all neighborhoods and communities. Zoning laws for mini pigs are different from state to state and from city to city. In some places, mini pigs are considered livestock and they cannot be kept in any area where livestock is not permitted. Contact the zoning department of the city or county where you live to see if zoning laws permit mini pig ownership. If you have a homeowner's association you will also have to check with them. If you are a renter, you need to be sure your lease allows for exotic pets.

THINGS TO THINK ABOUT IF YOU WANT A MINI PIG

- Do the zoning laws in your area allow you to own one?
- Mini pigs can spend some of their time indoors. They also need time outdoors with enough space to run, play, graze, and relieve themselves. Their outdoor area should have a place to rest, a fence, and shade for protection from the Sun.
- Mini pigs need health care from a veterinarian that is specially trained to work with farm animals. They need vaccinations and their hooves and teeth need regular care. A mini pig will need to be spayed or neutered in order to be a good pet.
- Mini pigs like to root and dig. These behaviors can cause damage to indoor and outdoor areas. Your house and yard need to be safe and able to withstand a strong, active animal.
- When you see a mini piglet, be aware that the tiny creature will grow to a much larger size.
- Mini pigs live for 15 years or more. Owning one is a long-term commitment.
- Mini pigs are social animals. They don't like to be left alone for long periods of time. When they get bored they may become destructive.
- Mini pigs need to be fed a special diet to stay healthy.
- Mini pigs need lots of time, training, and attention.
- It's important to consider if a mini pig will fit in with other pets in the household.

WEASELING ITS WAY INTO YOUR HEART

Have you ever heard of the weasel war dance? Have you ever been scared by a sofa monster? Have you ever encountered a carpet shark? Does the crocodile roll sound like fun? Meet the funny, furry little critter that can show you all of these tricks: the ferret.

FUN FACTS

When ferrets get excited and want to play, they hop sideways, leap, and bounce. Ferret owners call this the weasel war dance.

Ferrets are mammals and part of the weasel family. This family includes minks, otters, badgers, wolverines, and polecats. Only ferrets are kept as pets. Ferrets are carnivores and closely related to skunks. Like their stinky relatives, ferrets have scent glands under their tail. They give off a bad smell to scare away enemies.

FUN FACTS

The black-footed ferret is a wild relative of the domesticated ferret. It is an endangered species that lives in the western United States.

MINK

OTTER

WOLVERINE

BADGER

BLACK-FOOTED FERRET

Ferrets' bodies are long, strong, and flexible. Their strength and flexibility comes from having unusually long vertebrae in their spines. Their bodies are supported by short legs that allow them to crawl through small spaces. They have straight tails and each foot has five toes with claws.

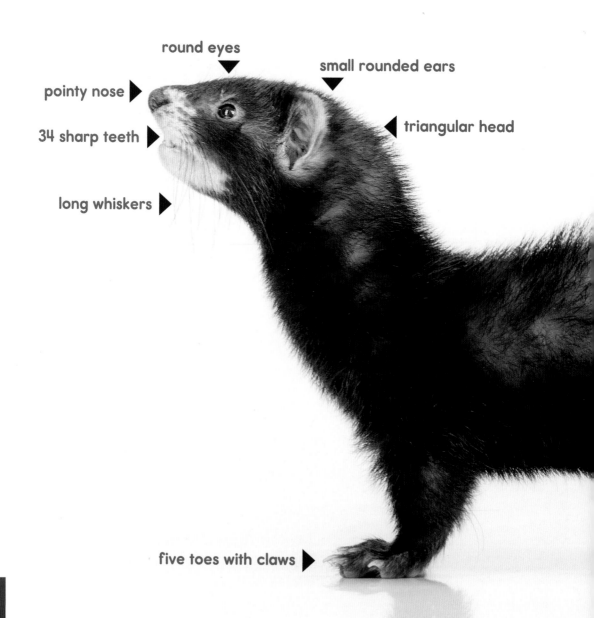

round eyes

small rounded ears

pointy nose ▶

34 sharp teeth ▶

◀ triangular head

long whiskers ▶

five toes with claws ▶

Ferrets have triangular shaped heads. They have small, rounded ears, round eyes, a pointy nose, and long whiskers. Ferrets have 34 sharp teeth, including four canine teeth like dogs and cats. Their eyesight is somewhat poor, but they are equipped with an excellent sense of smell and keen hearing.

FUN FACTS

kits: baby ferrets
hobs: adult males
jills: adult females
business: group of ferrets
hoblet: neutered male
sprite: spayed female

long vertebrae in spine ▼

◀ straight tail

◀ short legs

Unlike cats and dogs, there is only one breed of domestic ferret. But within that breed, ferrets vary in coat color and markings. A ferret may have a mask across its face, a bib of color on its chest, or a blaze of color down its back. Some ferrets have a color pattern similar to a panda. Their fluffy coats have two layers: outer protective hairs and an undercoat.

FUN FACTS

The word ferret comes from a Latin word, furittus, which means little thief.

Ferret Colors	Guard Colors	Undercoat	Eyes	Nose	Photo
albino	white to cream	white to cream	ruby red	pink	
black	true black	white or slight golden	black	solid or speckled black	
black sable	dark blackish brown	white to cream	dark brown or black	solid or speckled blackish brown	
champagne	tan or light chocolate	white to cream	dark brown or black	beige, pink, or pink with a beige or light brown t-outline	
chocolate	milk chocolate brown	white or slight golden	brown or burgundy	pink, beige, brick, or with a light brown t-outline	
dark-eyed white	white to cream	white to cream	burgundy	pink	
sable	warm, deep brown	white, cream, or light golden	brown or black	light brown, speckled brown, or with a brown t-outline	

THE FERRET'S PLACE IN HISTORY

Ferrets are not wild animals. They were domesticated about 2,500 years ago. Scientists believe they are descendants of the European polecat. People started keeping ferrets thousands of years ago in ancient Greece. They used them for ferreting other small animals out of their holes. Ferrets could catch small game or chase it into the hands of a waiting hunter.

▶▶ Ferreting with muzzled ferrets is described in Livre de Chasse, or Book of the Hunt, written by Count Gaston Phoebus of France in 1387.

When people traveled from Europe to the New World, ferrets came along on ships to kill mice. In North America, people started keeping ferrets in the 17th century. Wherever grain was stored, rodents came to feast. Ferrets helped eliminate pesky rats and mice. The pet ferret fad started in the United States in the 1980s. People liked their small size and playful personalities. They could be kept in small spaces and trained to use litter boxes.

FUN FACTS

Ferrets have a royal connection. German Emperor Frederick II and Mongolian leader Ghengis Khan kept ferrets for hunting.

GENGHIS KHAN
CIRCA 1227

FREDERICK II
1194-1250

A FERRET LIFE FOR ME

Ferrets are small and quiet like cats. They are playful and affectionate like dogs. They have funny, lovable personalities. They dance around, pounce on shoes, play hide-and-seek, and chase anything that rolls. Their energy can seem limitless.

Ferrets play hard and sleep hard. They need between 15 and 20 hours of sleep each day. They sleep so deeply you might wonder if they are still alive! They typically sleep for a few hours, wake up, eat, go to the bathroom, play, then sleep some more.

FUN FACTS

More about Hobs and Jills
Male ferrets are always bigger than female ferrets.
- **weight:** females 1-3 pounds (0.5-1.4 kilograms); males 3-5 pounds (1.4-2.3 kilograms)
- **length:** females 12-16 inches (30-41 centimeters); males 16-24 inches (41-61 centimeters)
- **lifespan:** females 6-10 years; males 7-10 years

The inquisitive ferret likes to crawl into small spaces. Drawers, shopping bags, and boxes are favorite hiding places. Ferrets have some mischievous ways. They like to take small objects or toys and hide them. Owners fondly call them sofa monsters and carpet sharks because they like to hide in sofa cushions and crawl under rugs. Ferrets speak a unique language. A soft barking noise referred to as dooking is its happy sound. A scared ferret will hiss. An upset ferret will squeak or scream.

Ferrets love and need attention from their owners. They become very attached to their humans. They also enjoy playing games and sleeping with other ferrets.

Ferrets can become friends with cats and dogs. They are natural hunters, so small pets such as hamsters, gerbils, and reptiles should not be kept around ferrets.

THE RIGHT PET?

Kits start their lives as part of a litter of six to ten baby ferrets. They are blind, deaf, and have no teeth. Like other mammals, they drink milk from their mother. Kits can leave their mother when they are between eight and 12 weeks old.

As new pets, kits need lots of time and attention. They begin to bond with their humans and learn their role in the family. Kits sleep a lot! When not sleeping, they will play and play.

▶▶ A newborn ferret is so small it can fit into a tablespoon. All kits have white fur when they are born.

FERRETS IN THE FAMILY

Ferrets need to live indoors. They prefer a cool area and a comfy cage. Cages should be large enough to provide a sleeping area and eating area. They also need a bathroom area. Ferrets can live by themselves, in pairs, or with a group.

Their sleeping area should have soft bedding. They like a place to hang out, such as a hammock.

Their eating area needs a sturdy food dish and a water bottle. Ferrets are meat eaters like cats and dogs. They eat a dry kibble that provides lots of protein. For treats, ferrets can eat cooked turkey or chicken. Ferrets need to eat frequently and they need lots of fresh water.

▶▶ Train your ferret to use a water bottle. They like to play in water, so having a bowl could get messy!

PET POINTERS

Fruits and vegetables should not be fed to a ferret. They are unable to digest any food that comes from plants.

Ferrets can be trained to use a litter box. The bathroom area should be away from the eating and sleeping areas. They eat a lot and go a lot! Their litter must be cleaned often.

The ferret's cage should be cleaned and disinfected weekly. Bedding and bowls need to be washed. This prevents sickness and helps control odors.

FUN FACTS

A healthy ferret has a thick, glossy coat. It has long whiskers and white teeth. Its eyes are bright and alert. Its nose is moist. It has a good disposition. It is alert, curious, and playful.

Important responsibilities go along with owning any pet. Just like dogs and cats, ferrets need care that is suited to their needs.

A happy, healthy ferret needs plenty of exercise and attention from its owner. Ferrets need to be out of their cages every day for four to six hours of exercise. They need playtime with their humans to go for walks and learn new tricks.

▶▶ Ferrets like to hide in small places, like a pocket, and crawl through tubes and tunnels.

Ferrets naturally have a light musky smell. This comes from glands in their skin. Clean bedding and a healthy diet help eliminate odor. Spaying or neutering also makes them less smelly. A bath every couple of months helps, too.

PET POINTERS

A veterinarian may need to perform an operation to remove a ferret's scent glands.

Veterinarians help keep ferrets healthy throughout their lives. Ferrets need to visit the veterinarian twice a year. The doctor will check their teeth to see if they need cleaning and check their ears for mites. Ferrets need yearly vaccinations against rabies and distemper. A veterinarian helps keep ferrets free of fleas and ticks.

PET POINTERS

Ferret Care
- Clean ears every two to three weeks
- Trim nails every two to three weeks
- Check teeth twice a year
- Get a bath every one to two months

FERRET FEATS

The friendly ferret can learn to do fun tricks. They love to hear their names and will come when called. They can be taught to sit up on their hind legs, play dead, and roll over — much like a dog. Ferrets can learn to walk on a leash attached to a special harness.

WALKING ON A LEASH

TUCK AND SCOOT

CROCODILE ROLL

SITTING UP

Many owners train their ferret to come when it hears a squeaky sound. They squeak a toy and reward the ferret for coming. It is important to teach them to come because they like to hide and it can be hard to find them.

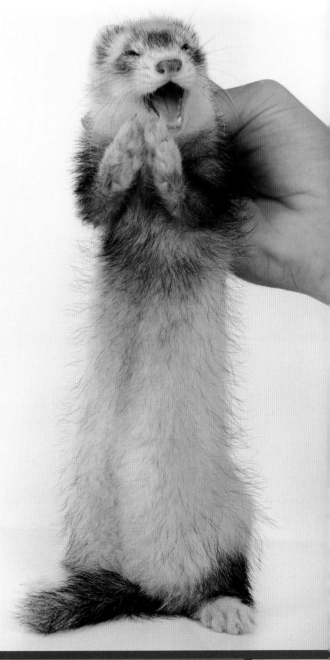

Training a ferret requires kindness and a gentle manner. Positive reinforcement works best. When they do something you want them to do, let them know it with a pat or a kiss.

Ferrets like to be rewarded with special treats such as a bit of egg. They also like to be rewarded with a favorite toy. Use praise and a positive tone of voice.

When your ferret misbehaves, let it know. Use a firm voice and say, "No!" Give it a timeout in a pet carrier. You can also correct misbehavior by picking it up by the loose skin on the back of its neck. This is called scruffing.

FUN FACTS

Ferret Power
Ferrets can perform an unusual function. Some have been trained to lead wires and cables through confined spaces to help with aircraft manufacturing and building construction. Lines are attached to their harnesses. They run along through narrow spaces or tunnels pulling lines along with them.

▶▶ **Use your thumb and first few fingers to hold your ferret firmly enough to immobilize it but not enough to hurt your pet.**

NO FERRETS ALLOWED?!

Cities and states have different laws about ferret ownership. At one time, ferrets were classified as wild animals that could not be legally kept as pets. Some of those laws still exist, but many restrictions have changed and ferret ownership is more widely accepted. Most places still require permits to breed ferrets.

Ferret ownership is illegal in California and Hawaii. California's Fish and Game Commission places them on a restrictive wildlife list. In Hawaii they are considered possible carriers of the rabies virus. Some cities such as Washington, D.C. and New York City restrict ferret ownership.

PET POINTERS

If you decide to add a ferret to your family, consider adopting one from an animal rescue organization.

DOES YOUR CITY OR STATE HAVE LAWS ABOUT FERRET OWNERSHIP?

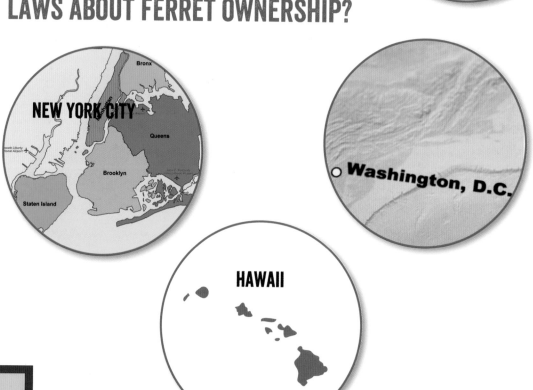

CALIFORNIA

NEW YORK CITY

Bronx

Queens

Brooklyn

Staten Island

Newark Liberty International Airport

Washington, D.C.

HAWAII

THINGS TO THINK ABOUT IF YOU WANT A PET FERRET

- A ferret owner must be willing to devote a lot of time to their pet.
- Ferrets can be smelly. They naturally give off a musky odor.
- Ferrets may nip their owners to get their attention or when they are startled.
- A ferret's home needs to be ferret-proofed to eliminate the places it could hide and get lost.
- Ferrets like to steal things and hide them. Small objects should be kept out of their reach.
- Ferrets like to chew. They can cause damage with their sharp teeth.
- Ferrets have difficulty living in temperatures above 85 degrees Fahrenheit (29 degrees Celsius).
- Ferrets need close supervision when they are out of their cages.
- Because of their body type and high activity level, a ferret may be difficult for a young child to handle.
- Ferrets can't be around smaller animals such as rabbits, hamsters, gerbils, and small reptiles.
- Ferrets have some unusual health problems. They are prone to some kinds of cancer. They can catch and transmit the flu.

GLOSSARY

bedding (BED-ing): material used for animals to cushion their bodies and absorb smells and wetness

canine (KAY-nine): pointed teeth on each side of the upper and lower jaw

carnivores (KAR-nuh-vorz): animals that eat meat

descendants (di-SEND-uhntz): those who can be traced to a particular individual or group

disinfected (diss-in-FEKT-id): cleaned for the purpose of killing germs

domesticated (duh-MESS-tuh-kate-id): tamed to live with or used by humans

inquisitive (in-KWIZ-i-tiv): extremely curious

kibble (KIB-uhl): coarsely ground dry food for animals

musky (MUHS-kee): an unpleasant animal odor

neutering (NOO-tur-een): a medical procedure that prevents male animals from reproducing

SHOW WHAT YOU KNOW

SKUNKS

1. Are skunks legal in your state?
2. What do skunks eat?
3. How do skunks communicate?
4. List three ways to keep your skunk safe.
5. What is the best way to play with a skunk?

WEBSITES TO VISIT

www.justskunks.com
www.skunkhaven.net/StatesForm.htm
www.skunk-info.org

BEARDED DRAGON

1. What are the challenges and benefits of having a bearded dragon for a pet?
2. Describe the proper home environment for a bearded dragon.
3. Explain the important nutritional requirements for bearded dragons.
4. How do bearded dragons communicate with each other?
5. Using the chart and photos on page 10, explain the similarities and differences between each type of bearded dragon.

WEBSITES TO VISIT

http://a-z-animals.com/animals/bearded-dragon
www.beardeddragonguide.com
www.thebeardeddragon.org

HEDGEHOG

1. How long have hedgehogs been on Earth?
2. Which part of the world do hedgehogs come from?
3. Name two facts about hedgehogs' quills.
4. When are hedgehogs least active?
5. Name three things a hedgehog needs in their home.

WEBSITES TO VISIT

www.coolkidfacts.com/hedgehog-facts-for-kids
www.kids.nationalgeographic.com/animals/hedgehog
www.hedgehogcentral.com/stats.shtml

PYGMY GOAT

1. Why do adult pygmy goats butt heads?
2. Where do pygmy goats originally come from?
3. How do horns keep pygmy goats cool?
4. What size shed fits two pygmy goats?
5. How should you care for a pygmy goat's hooves?

WEBSITES TO VISIT

www.marylandzoo.org/animals-conservation/mammals/pygmy-goat
https://www.oregonzoo.org/discover/animals/pygmy-goat
www.taytopark.ie/zoo/pygmy-goat

MINI PIG

1. Explain both the challenges and benefits of having a mini pig for a pet.
2. Describe the similarities and differences between having a mini pig for a pet and having a dog for a pet.
3. When did mini pigs become popular pets?
4. What is the average lifespan of a pet mini pig?
5. What are some things you must do to prepare before purchasing a mini pig?

WEBSITES TO VISIT

http://cincinnatizoo.org/blog/animals/mini-juliana-pig/
www.dogonews.com/2009/10/8/teacup-piglets
www.pigs4ever.com

FERRET

1. What makes a ferret unique?
2. What responsibilities are required in the day-to-day care of a pet ferret?
3. How can you keep a ferret healthy throughout its lifetime?
4. Ferrets have been kept by humans for different reasons over the course of history. Identify the reasons and explain how ferret ownership has changed over time.
5. What are the benefits and challenges of having a ferret for a pet?

WEBSITES TO VISIT

www.humanesociety.org/animals/ferrets
www.a-z-animals.com/animals/ferret
www.ferret.org/read/faq.html

MEET THE AUTHORS

ABOUT THE AUTHOR

Ann H. Matzke has an MFA in writing for children and young adults from Hamline University. She grew up loving animals and had many different kinds of pets: cats, fish, turtles, hamsters, gerbils and even fire-bellied toads. Ann and her family live in Gothenburg, Nebraska, with their Labradors, Penny and Lucy, and three cats, Max, Michael, and Foggy Nelson. Ann enjoys traveling, reading, and photography.

ABOUT THE AUTHOR

Cristie Reed is a literacy teacher and lifelong animal lover. She enjoys caring for pets. In her lifetime she has owned and cared for three pet goats, a few chickens, a few ducks, a green snake, two anole lizards, a guinea pig, a pony, a caiman, a squirrel, three cats, eight dogs, and one very special peacock. She lives in Florida with her husband and miniature schnauzer, Rocky.

ABOUT THE AUTHOR

Karen Latchana Kenney is an author and editor in Minneapolis, Minnesota. She has written dozens of books for kids on many topics, from how stars and galaxies form to how to care for pet sugar gliders. Her award-winning books have received positive and starred reviews in Booklist, School Library Connection, and School Library Journal. When she's not researching and writing books, she loves biking and hiking Minnesota's state parks, traveling to new and exciting places with her husband and son, and gazing up at the night sky in northern Minnesota at her family's cabin, where the stars are vividly bright. Visit her online at http://latchanakenney.wordpress.com

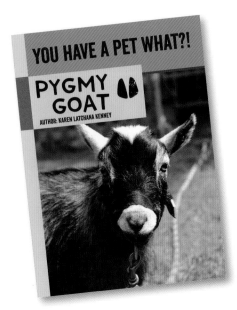

YOU HAVE A PET WHAT?!

PYGMY GOAT
AUTHOR: KAREN LATCHANA KENNEY